Nature Spotting
Russell Weekes

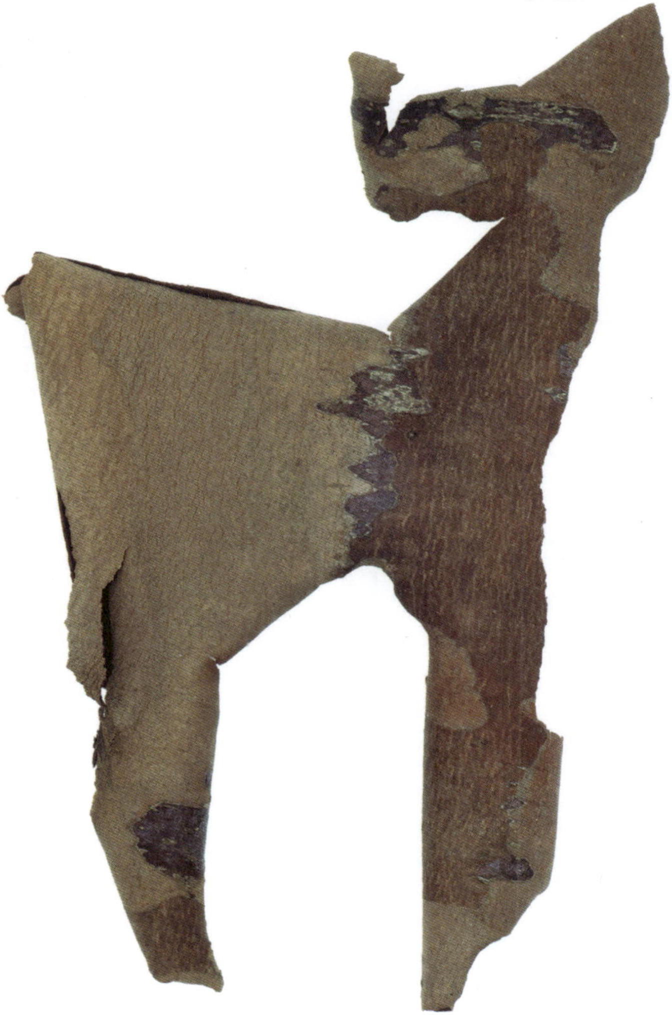

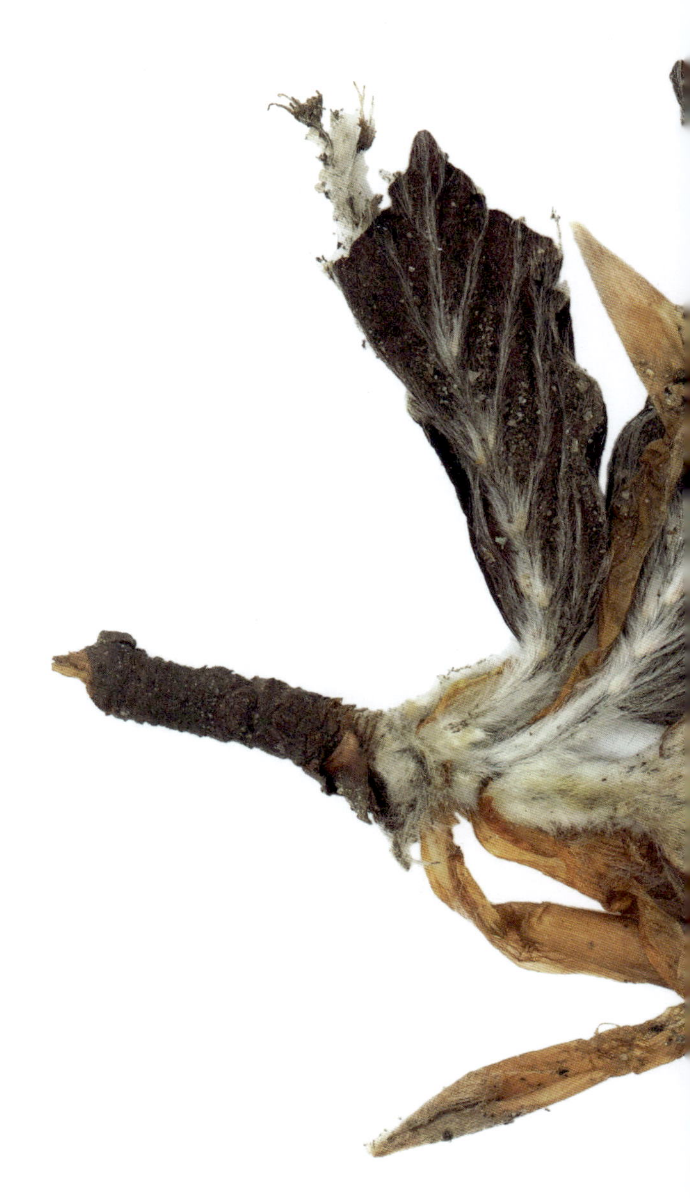

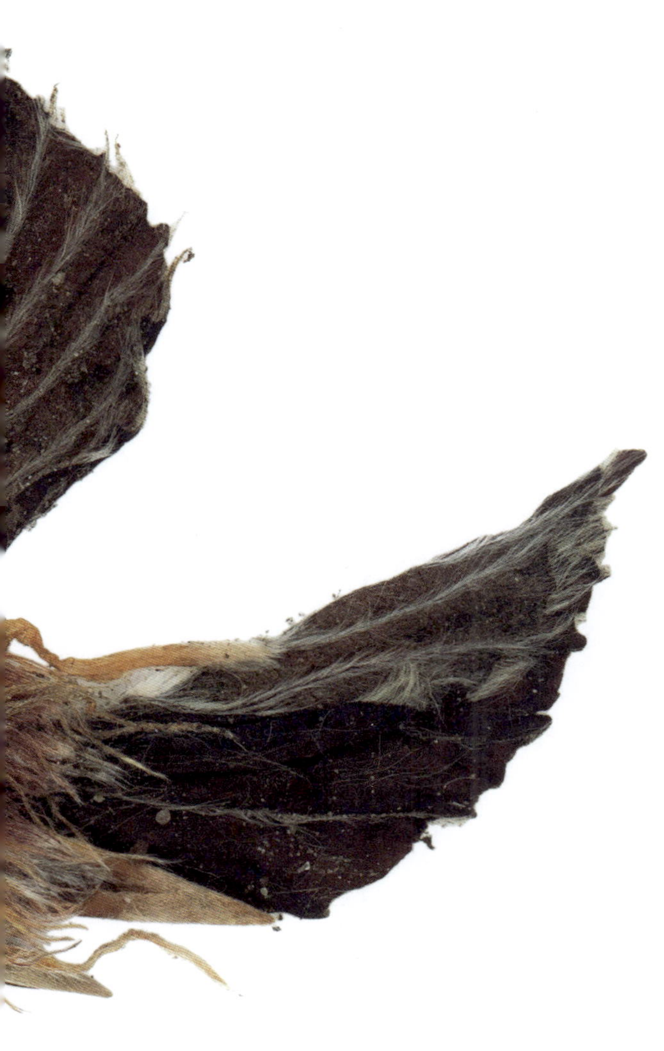

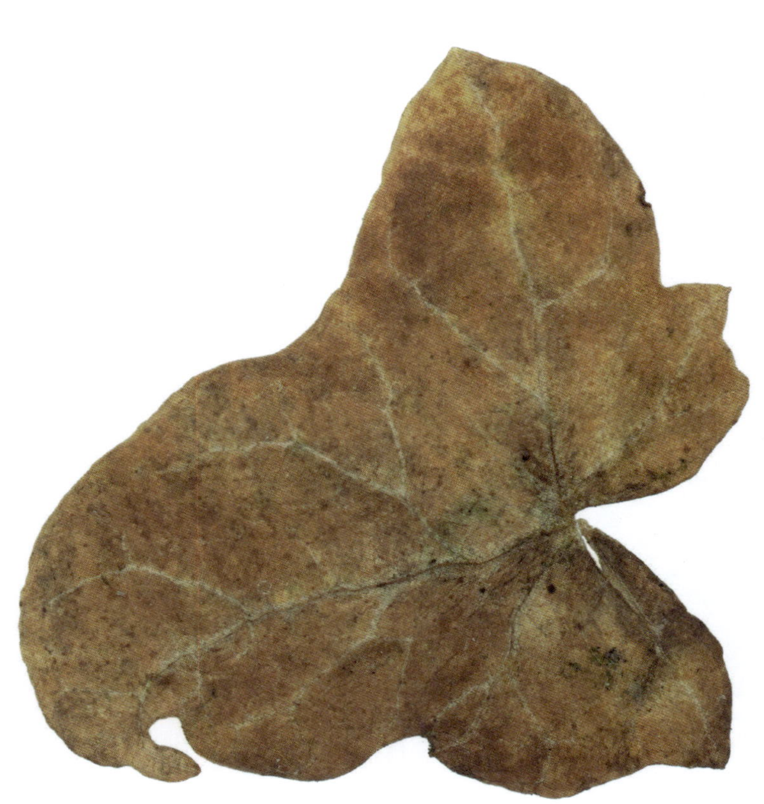

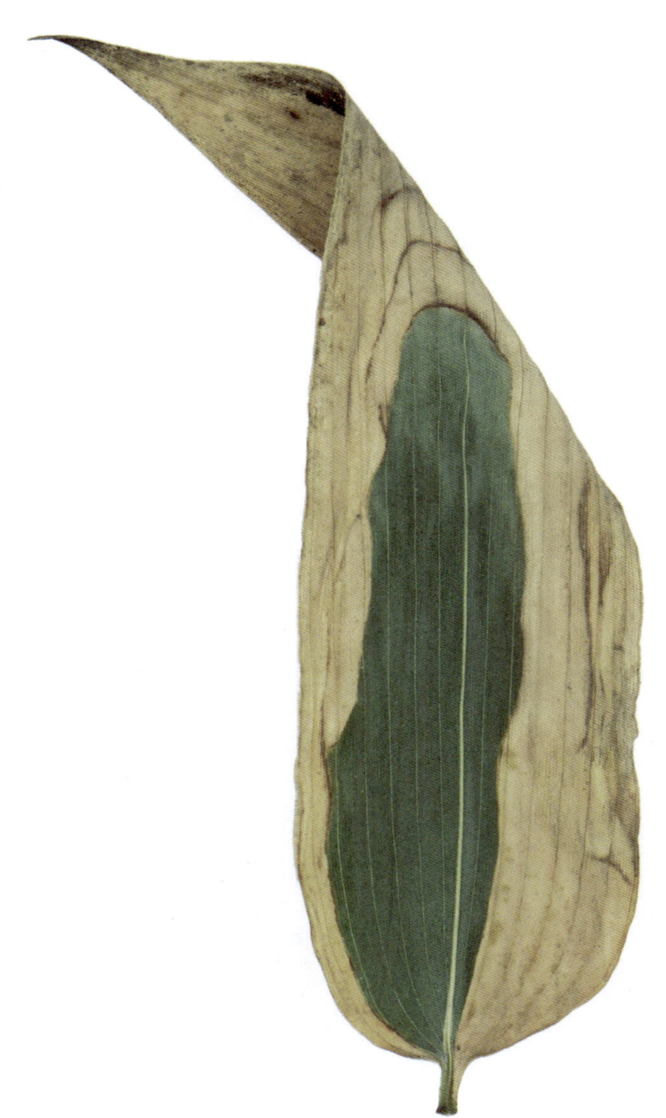

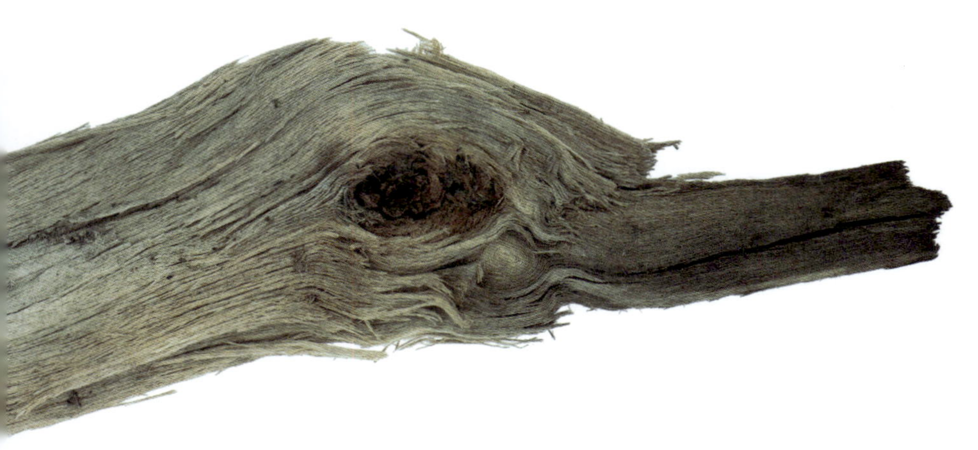

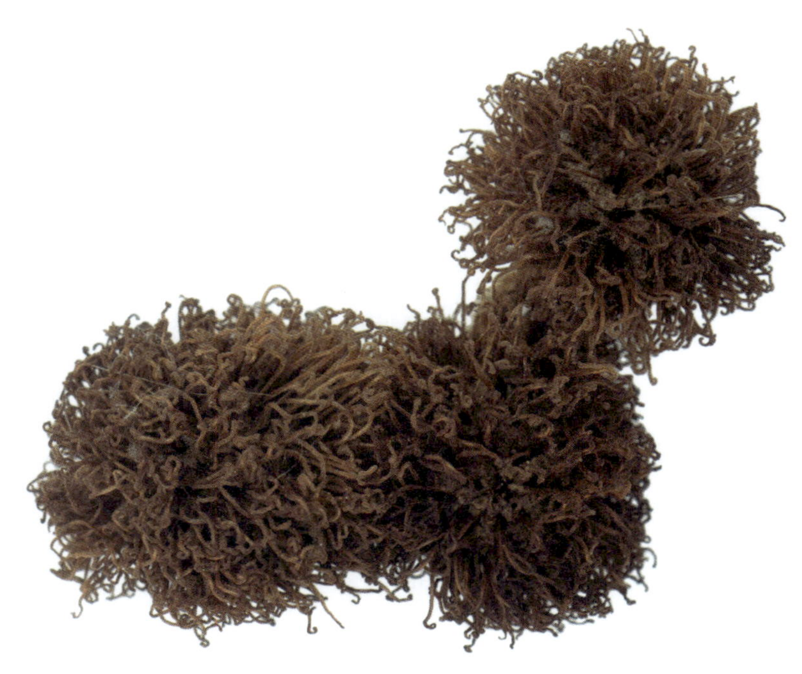

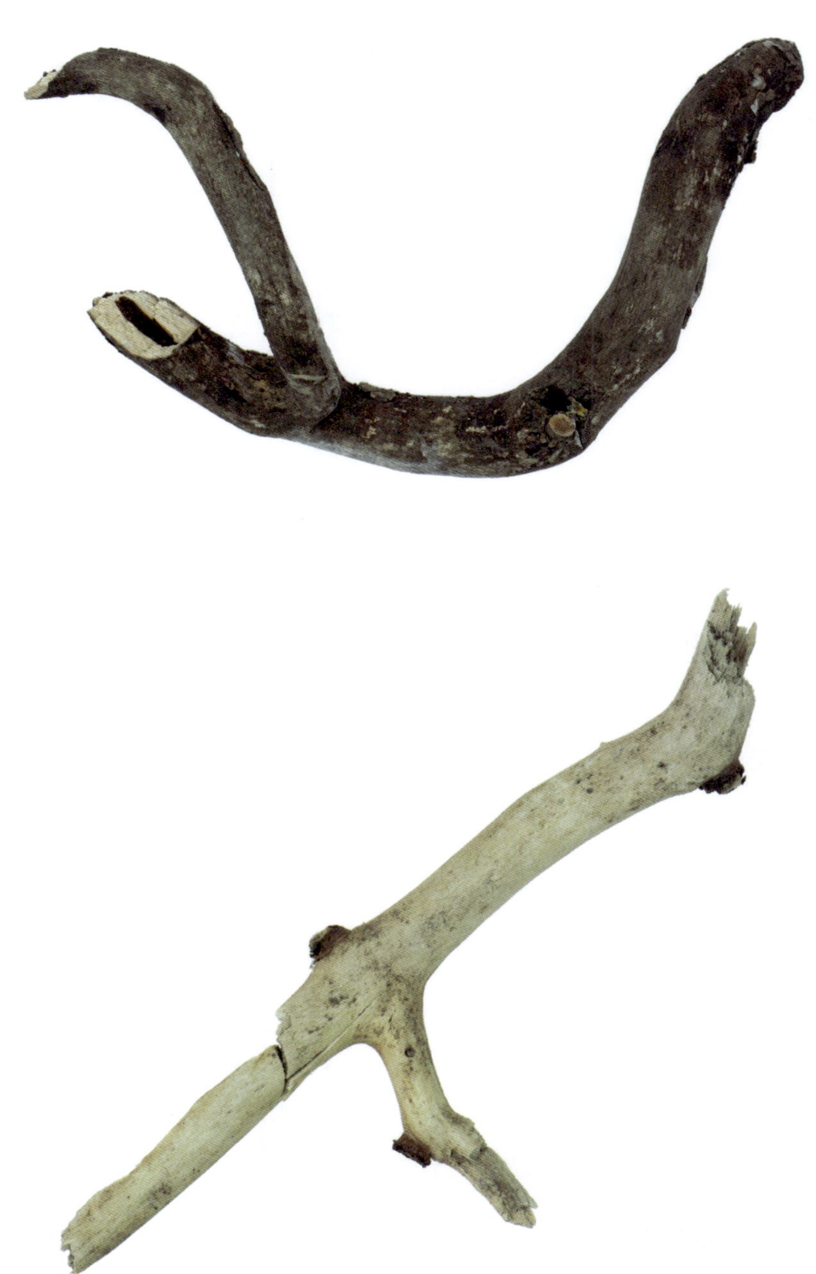

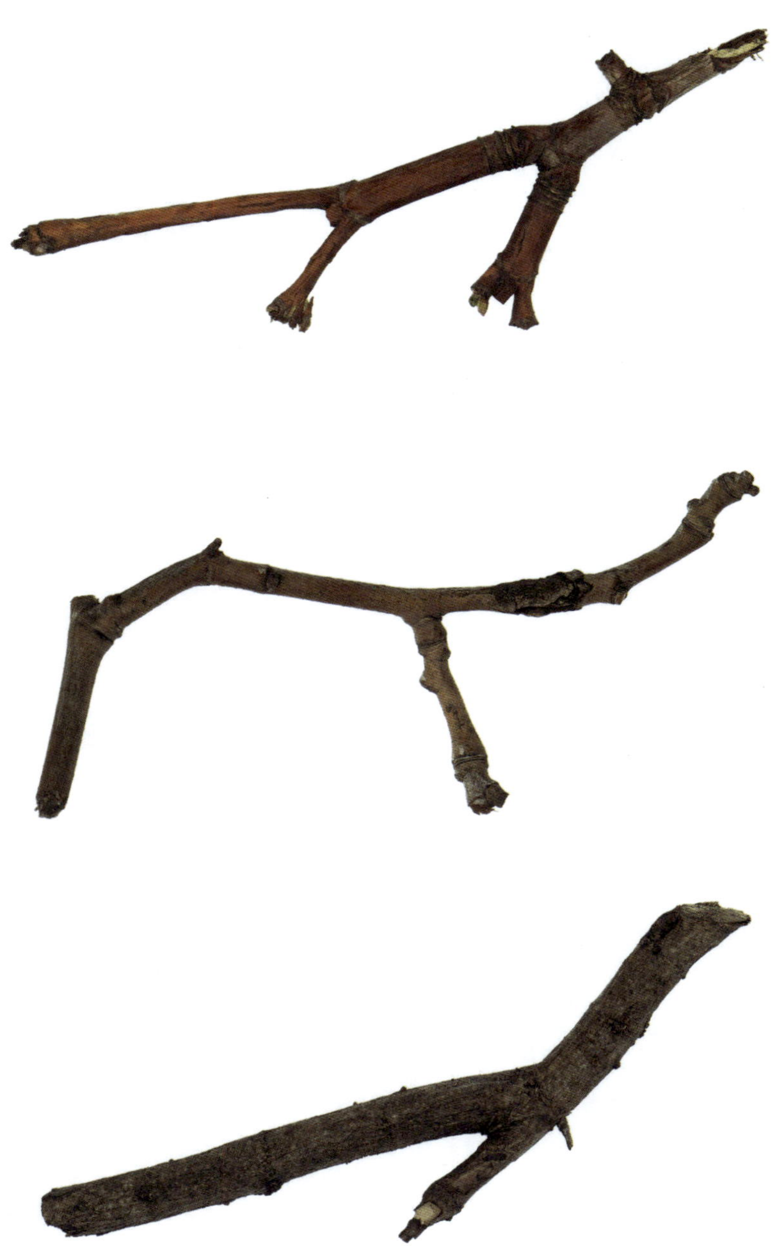

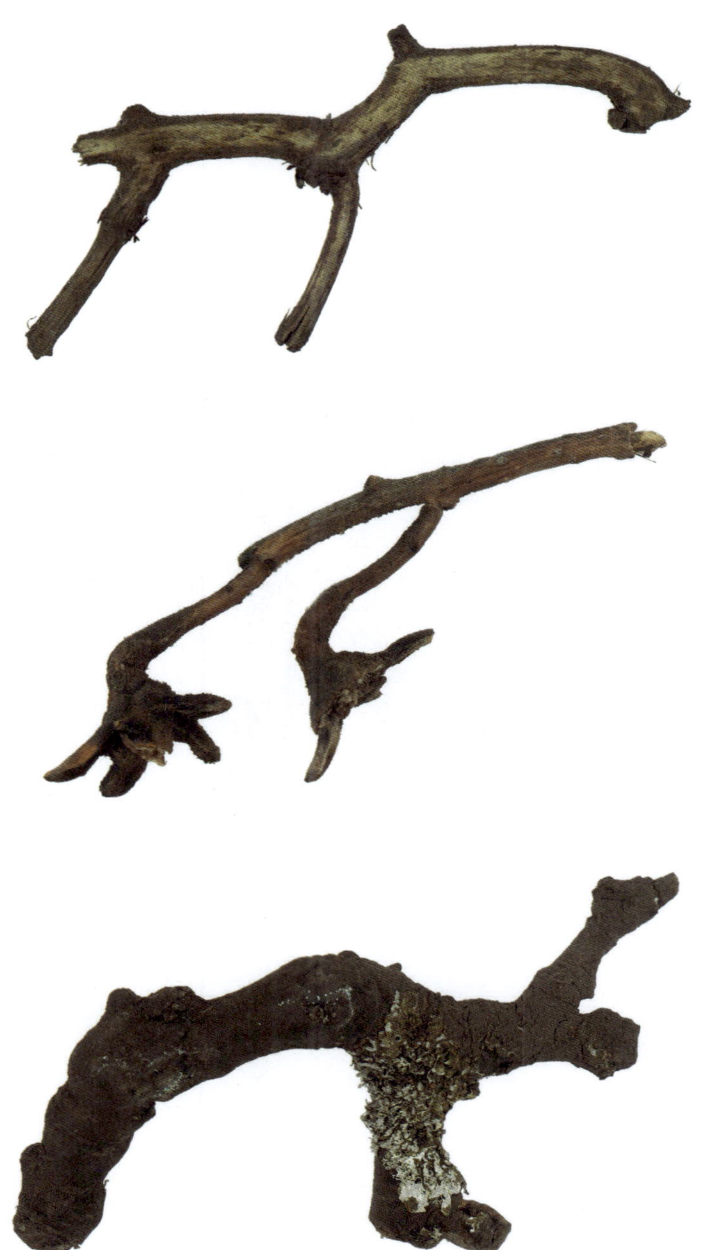

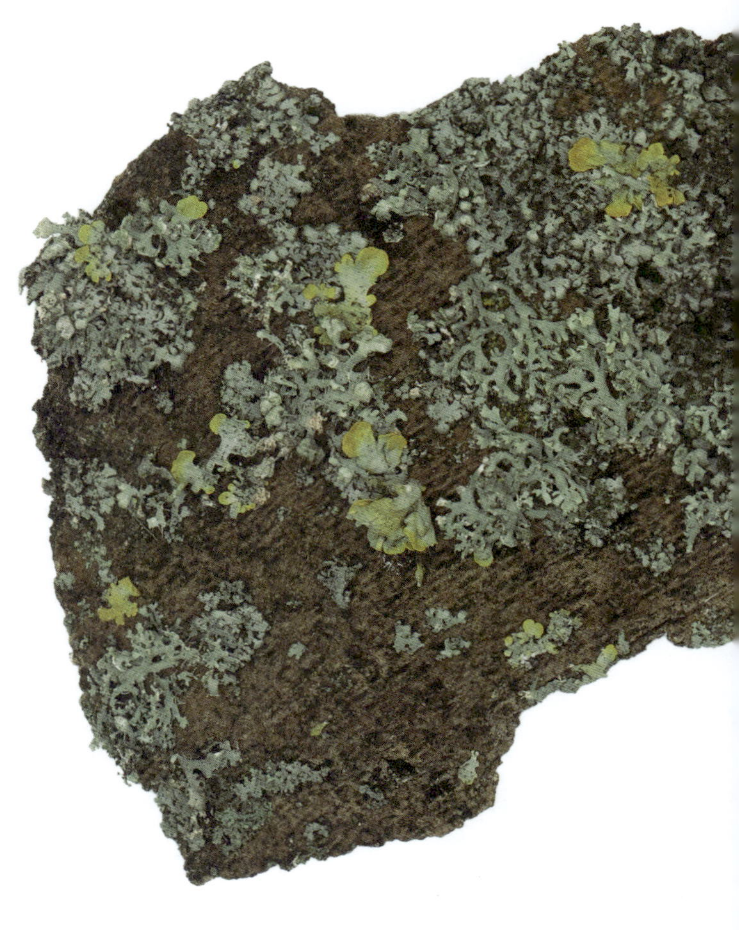

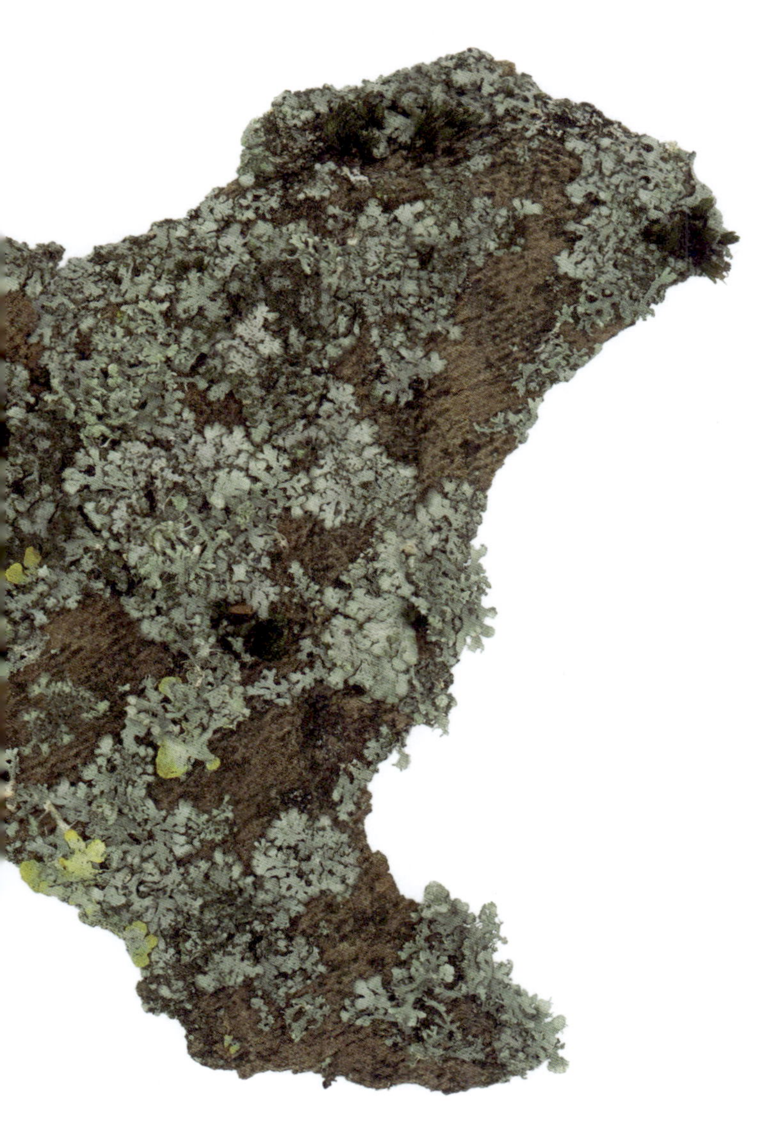

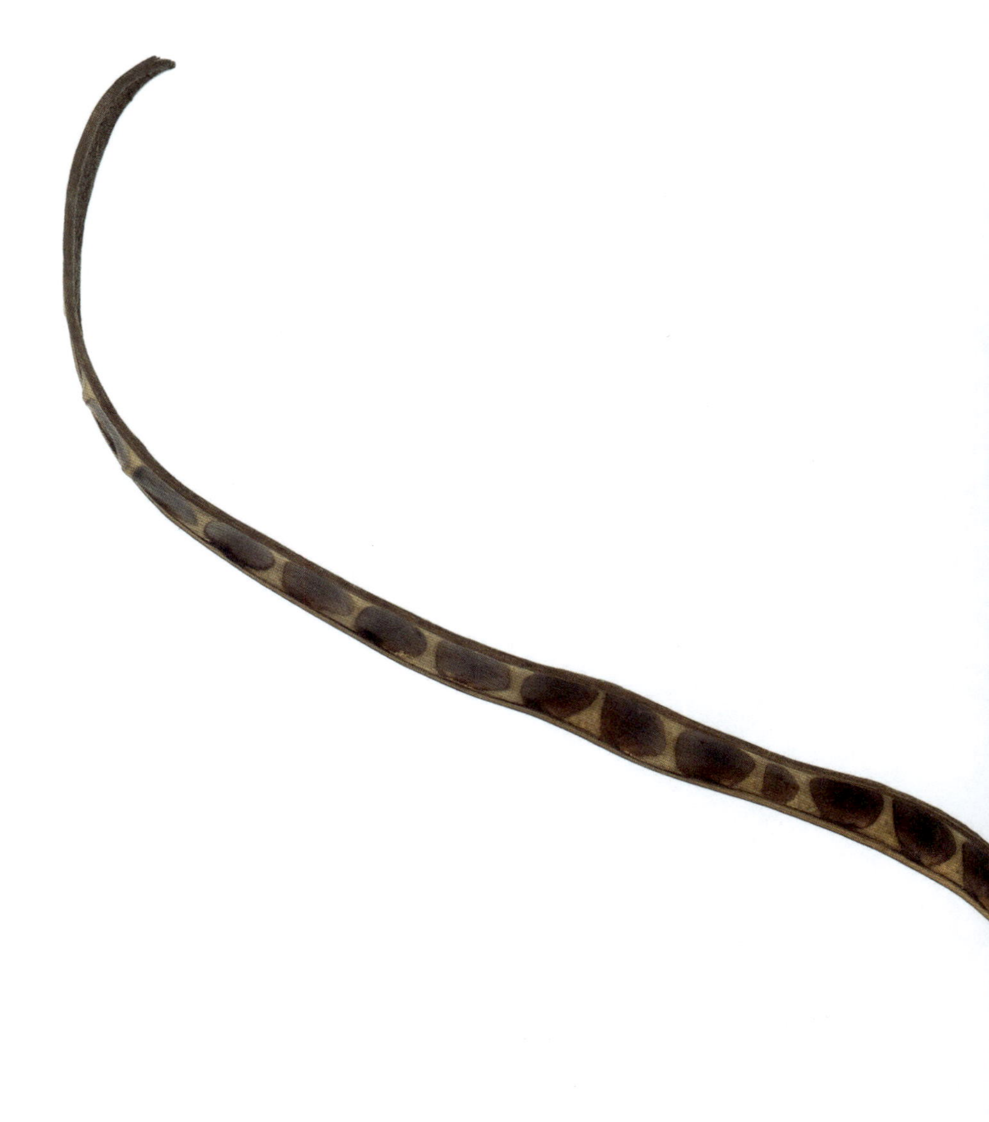

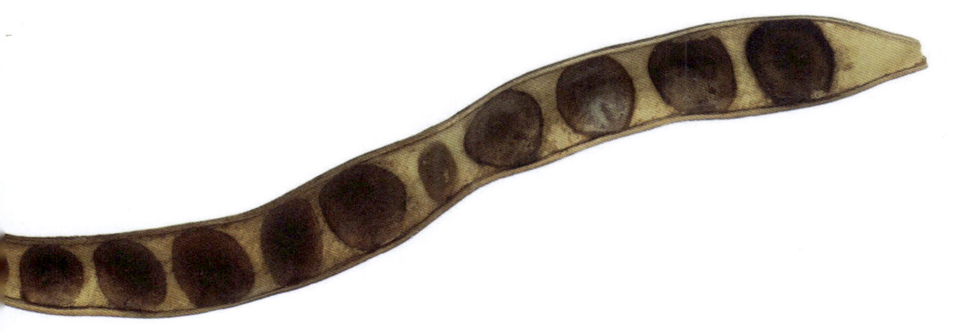

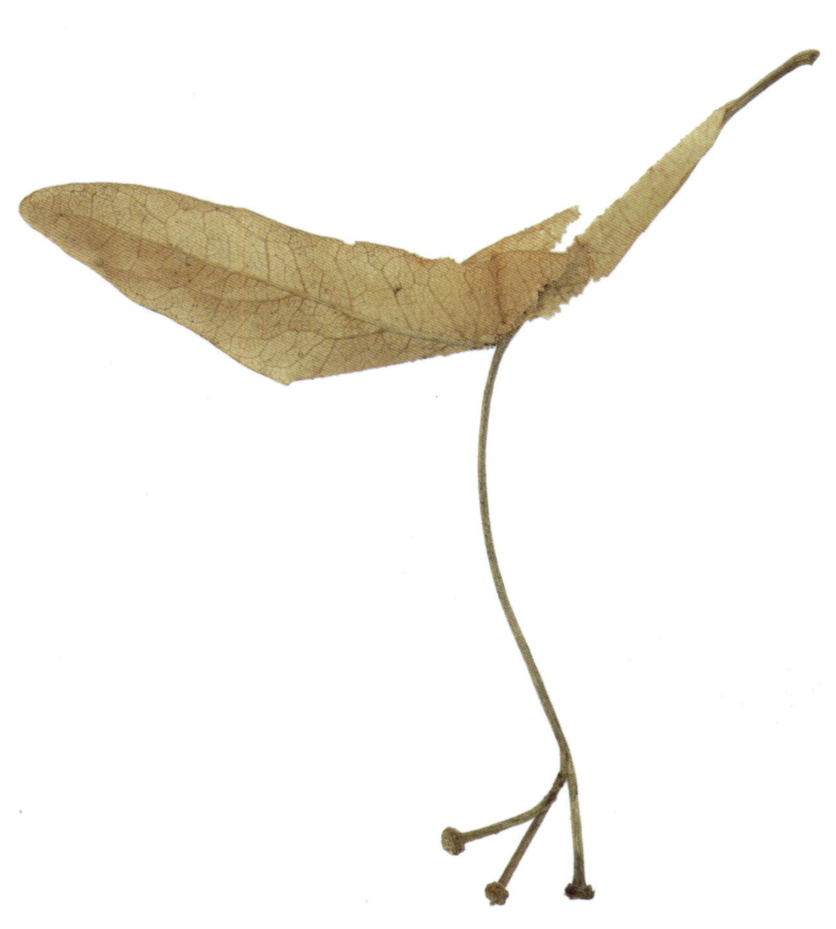

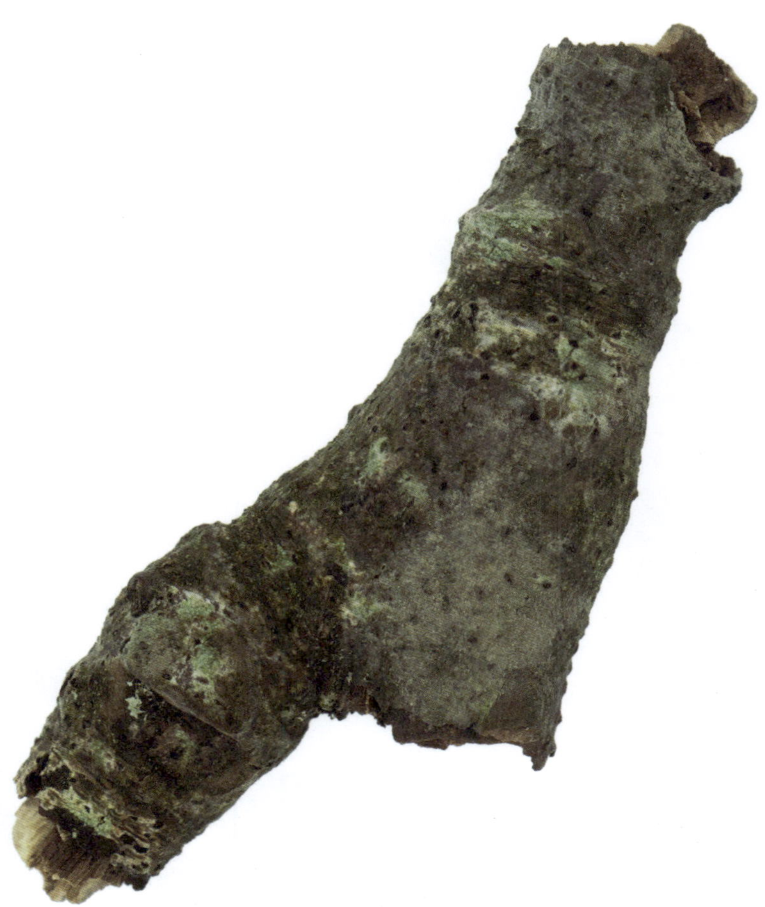

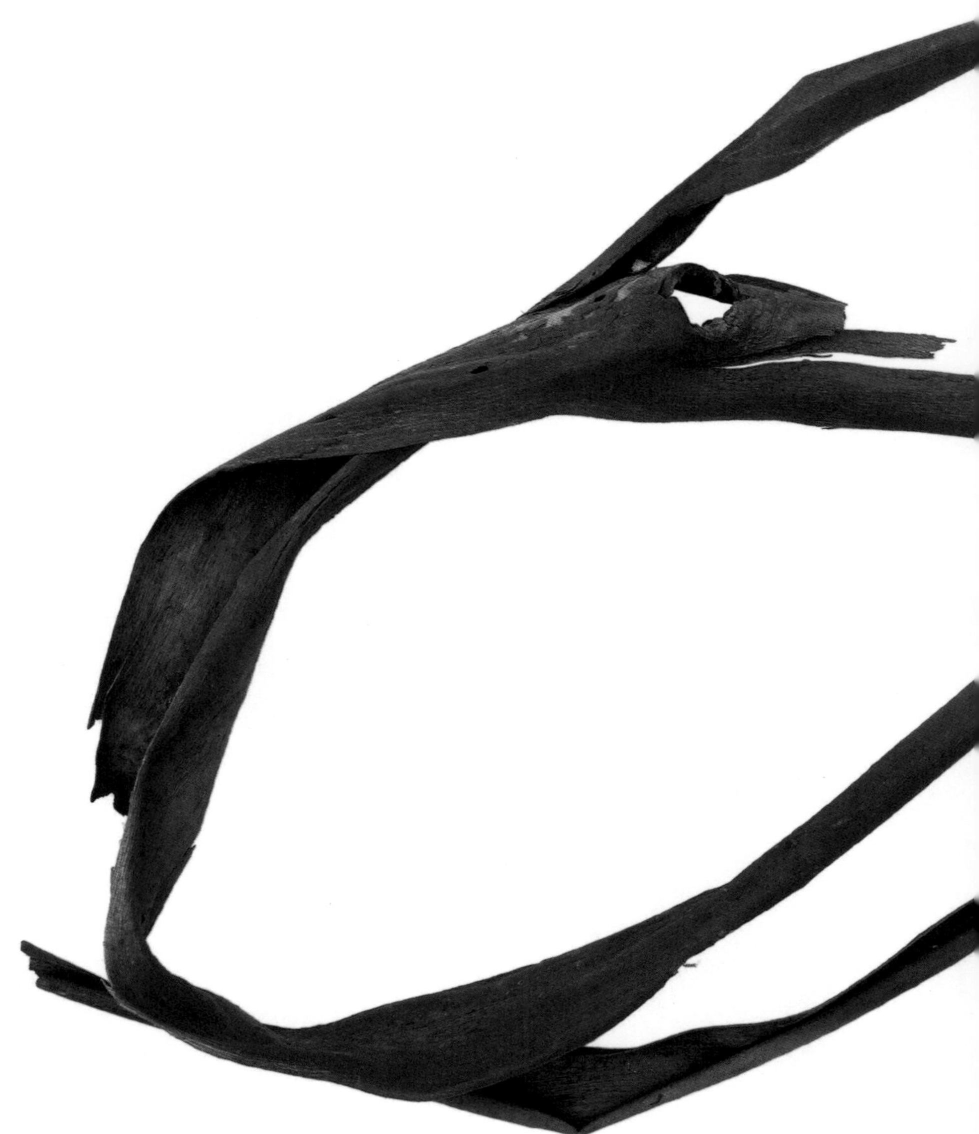

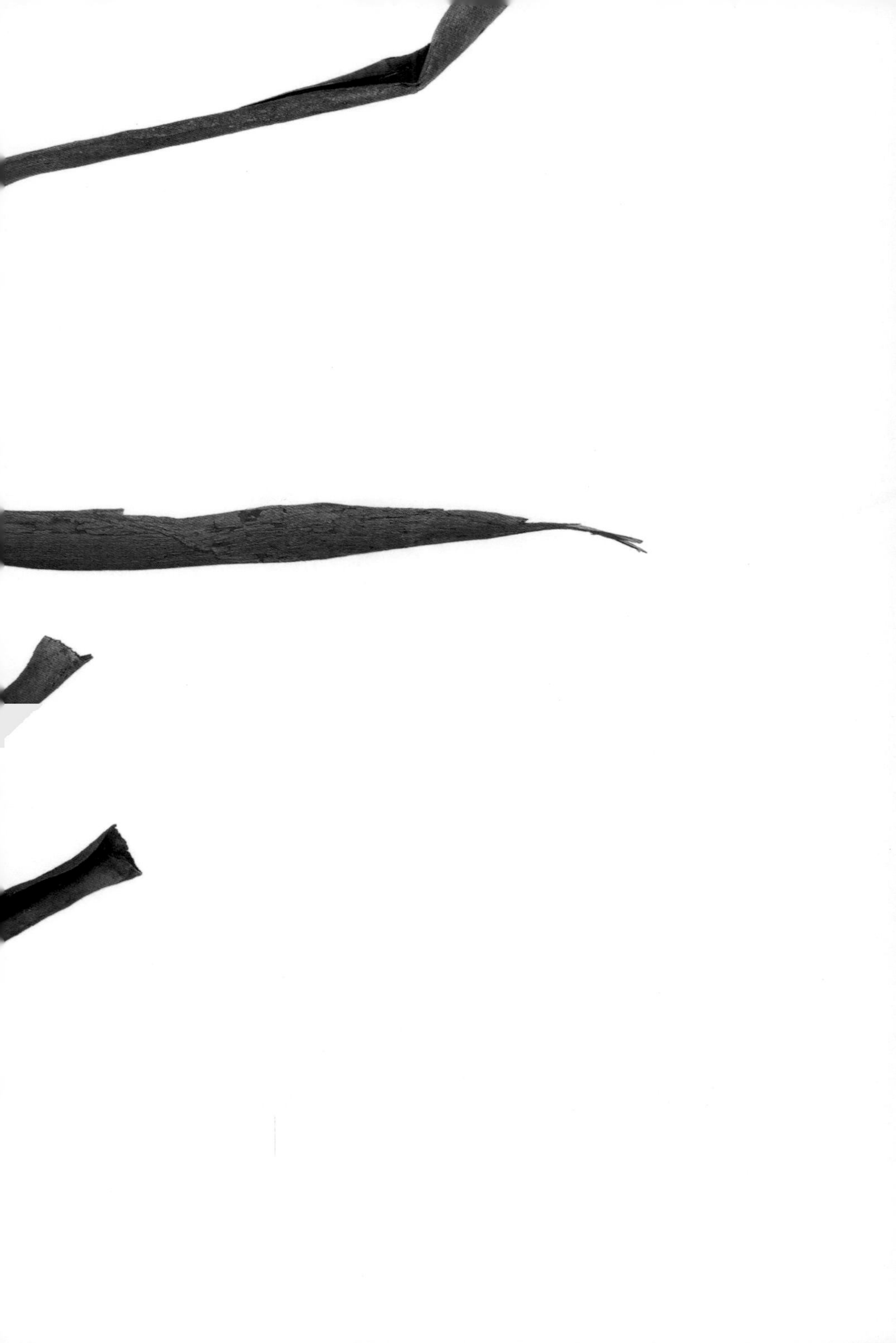

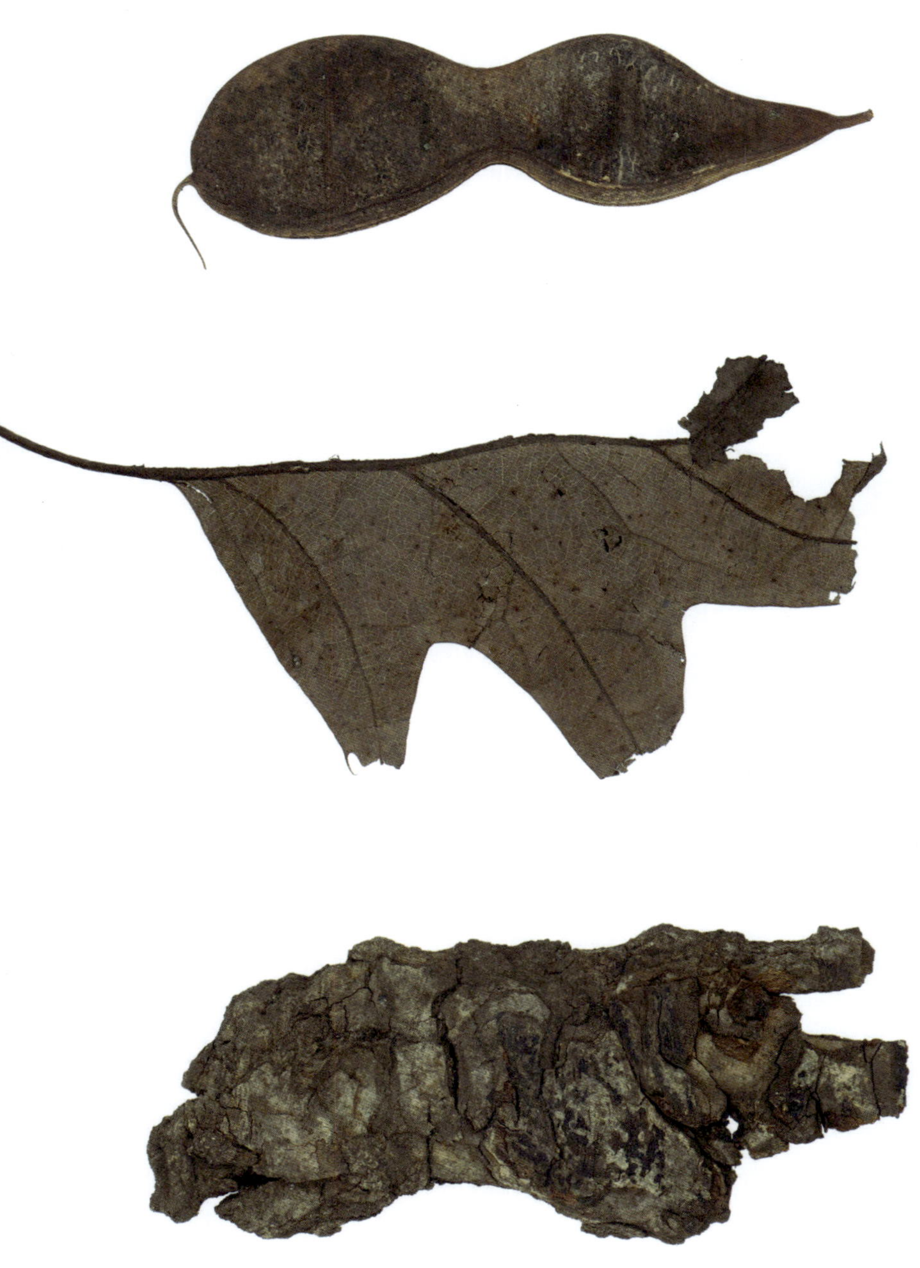

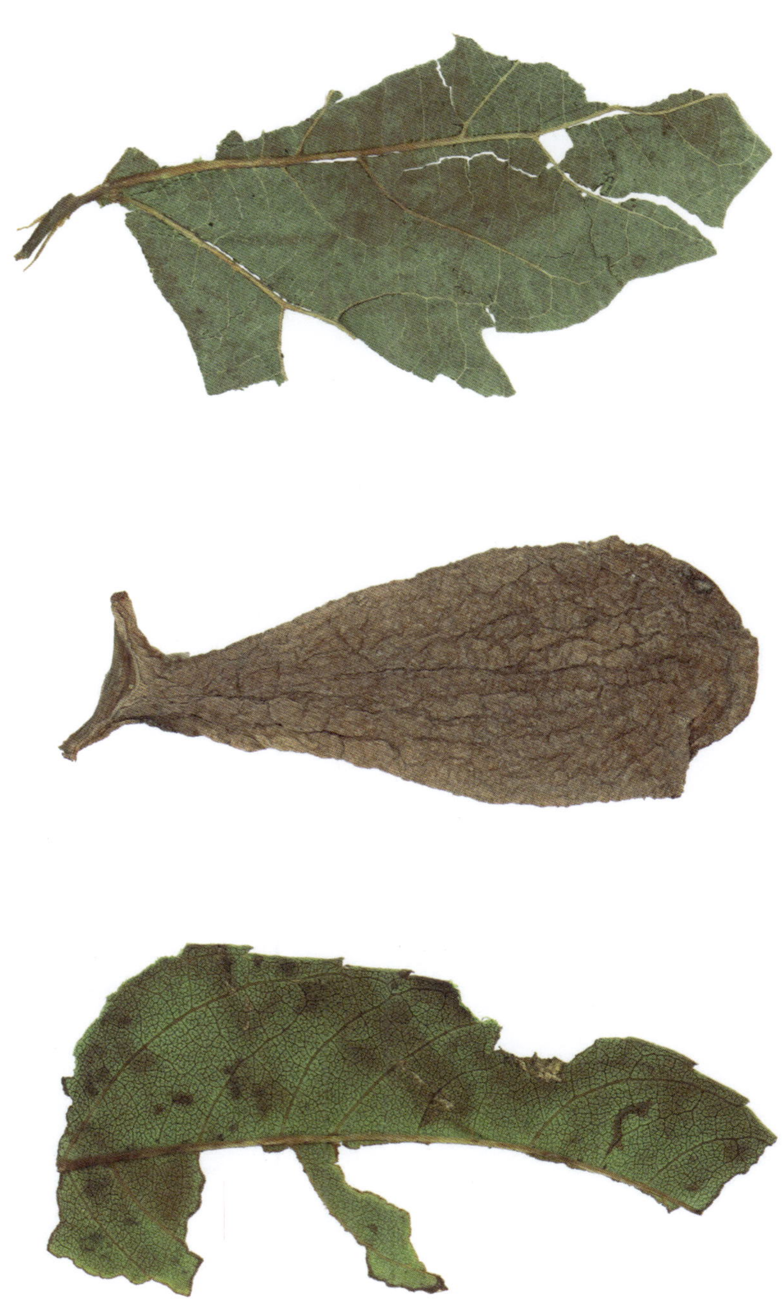

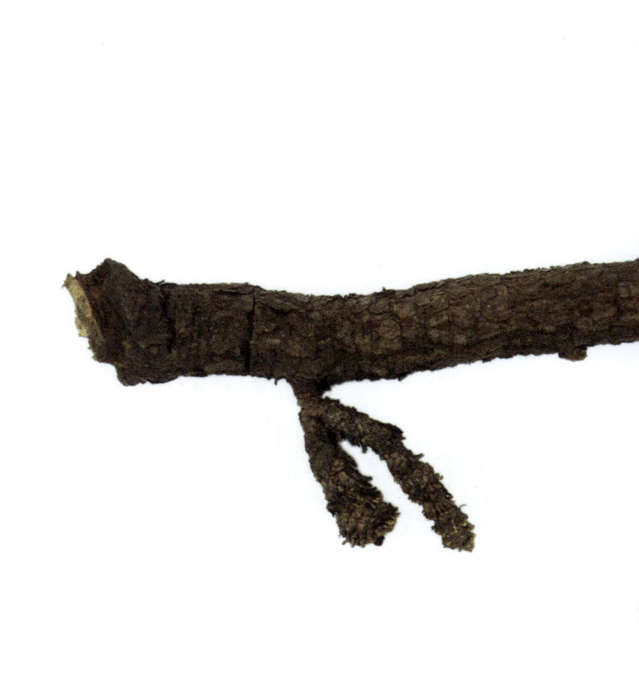

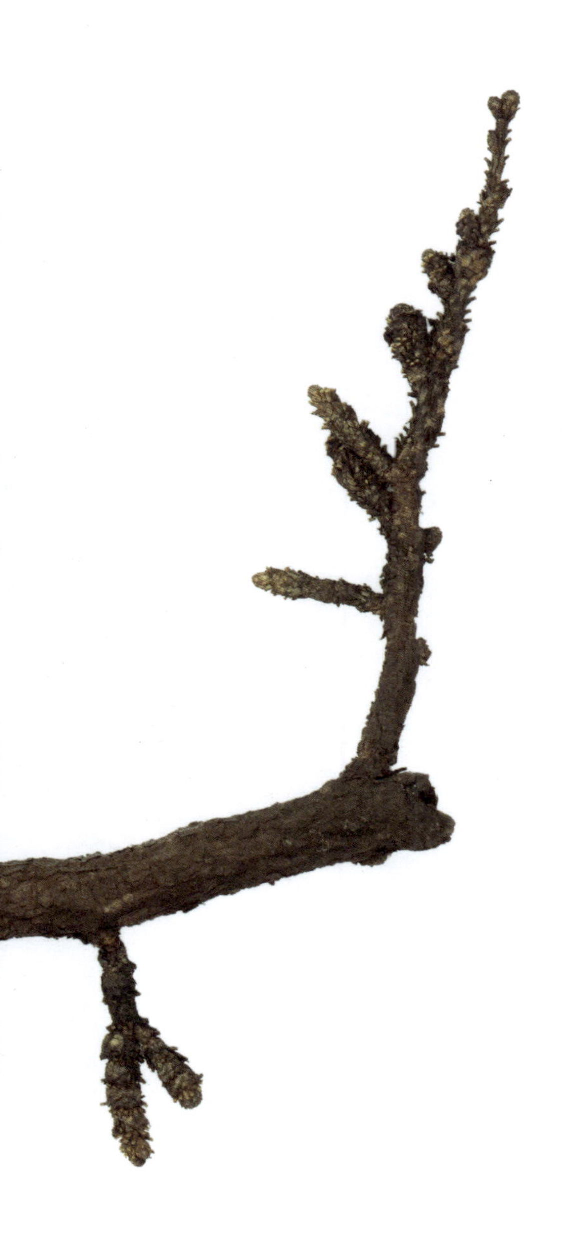

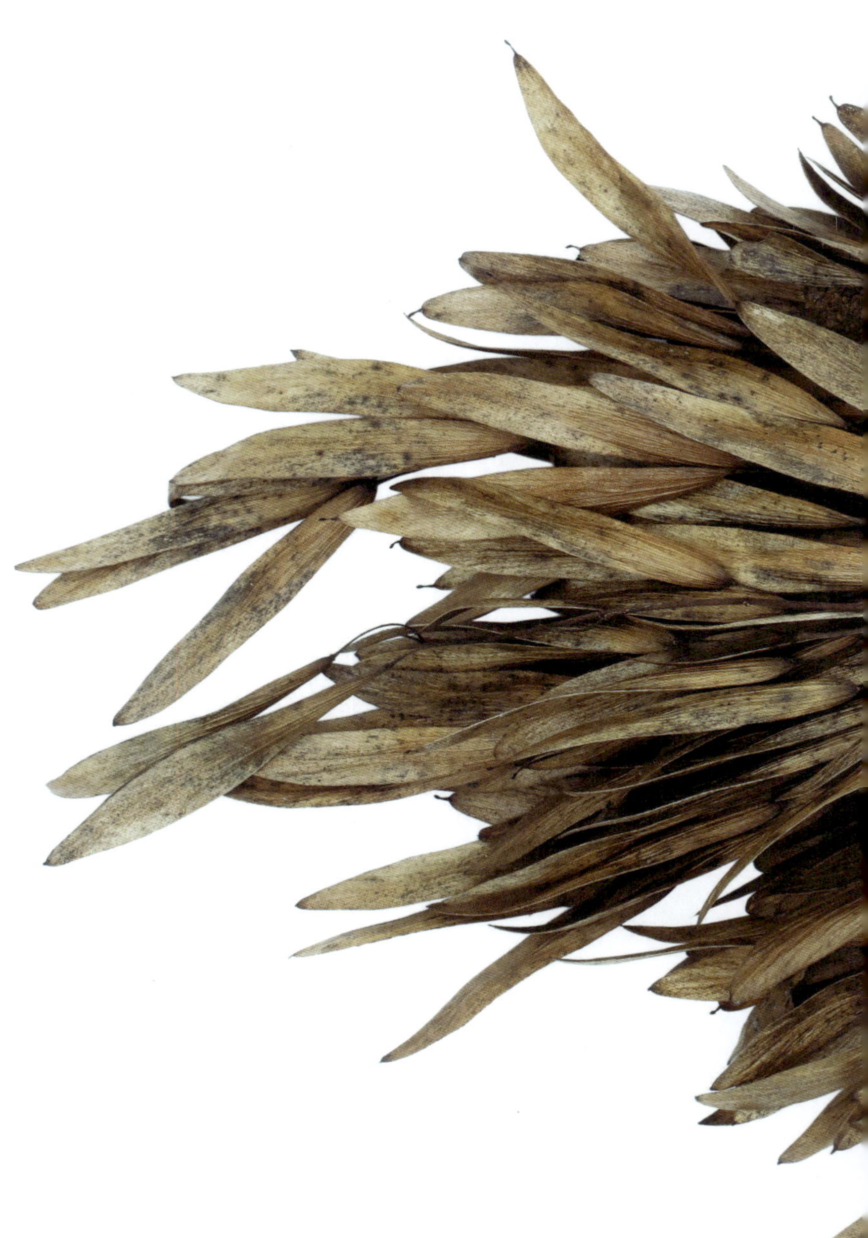

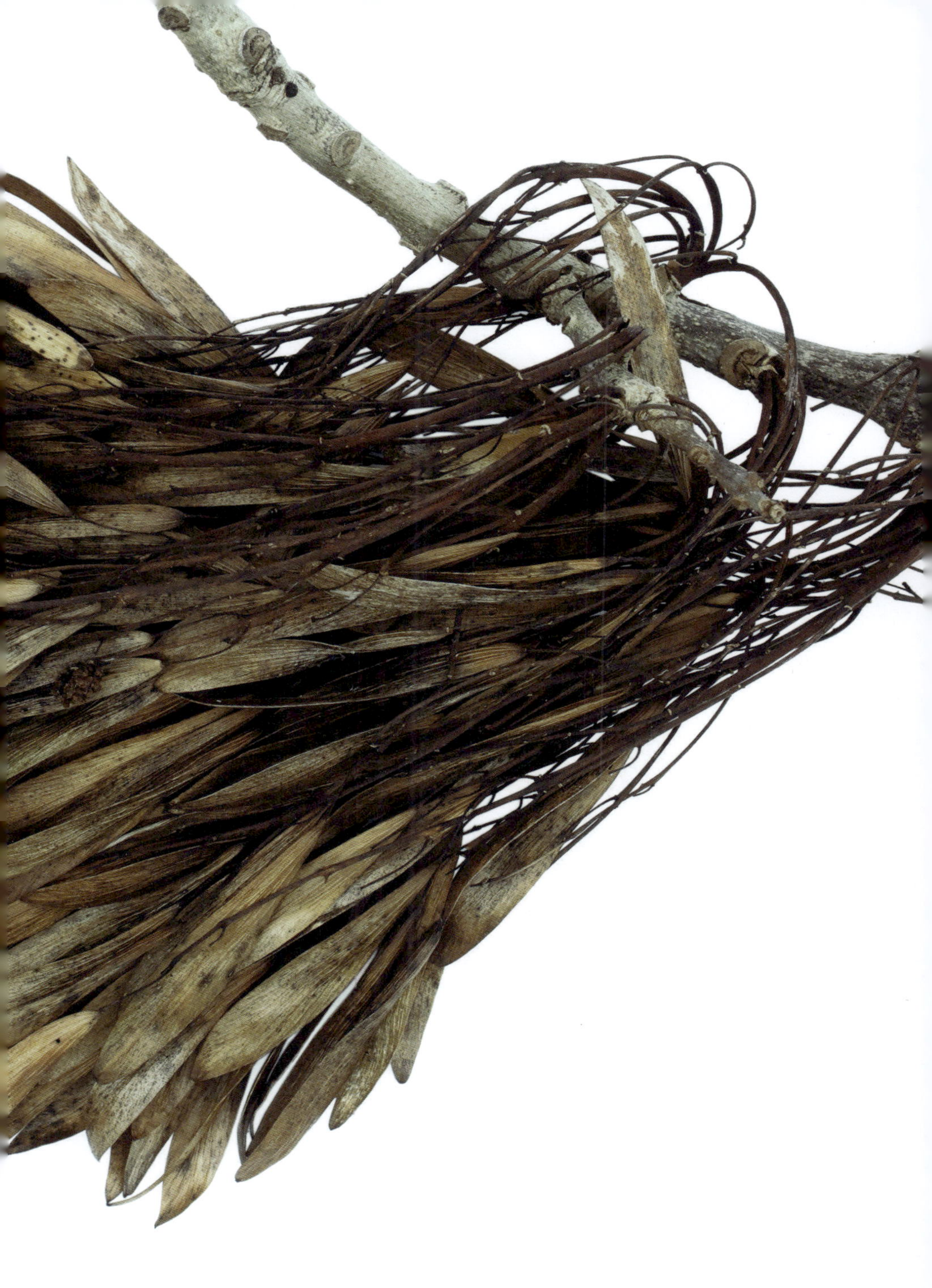

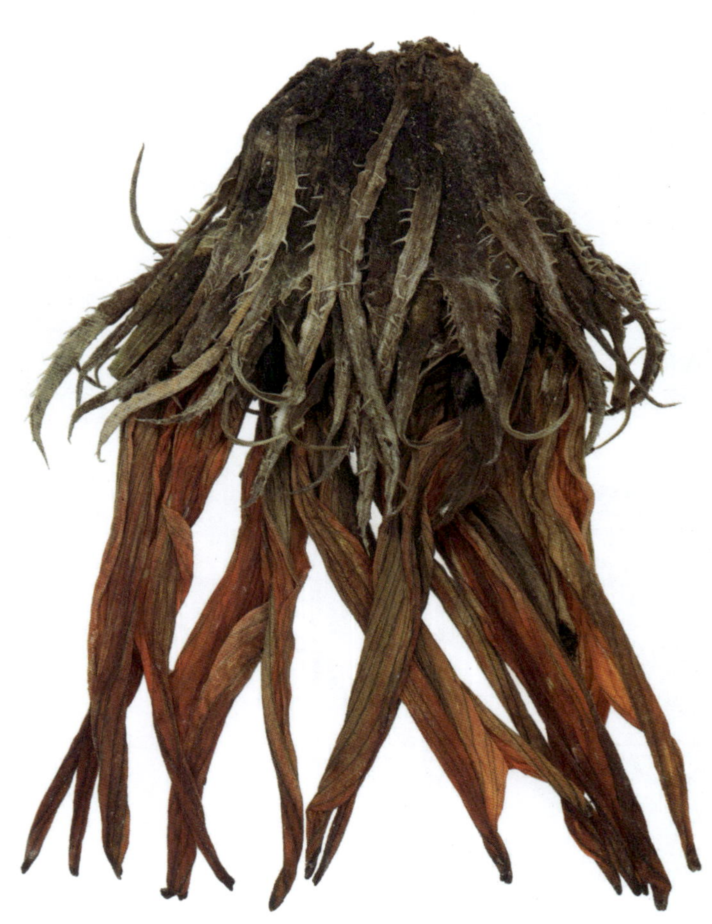

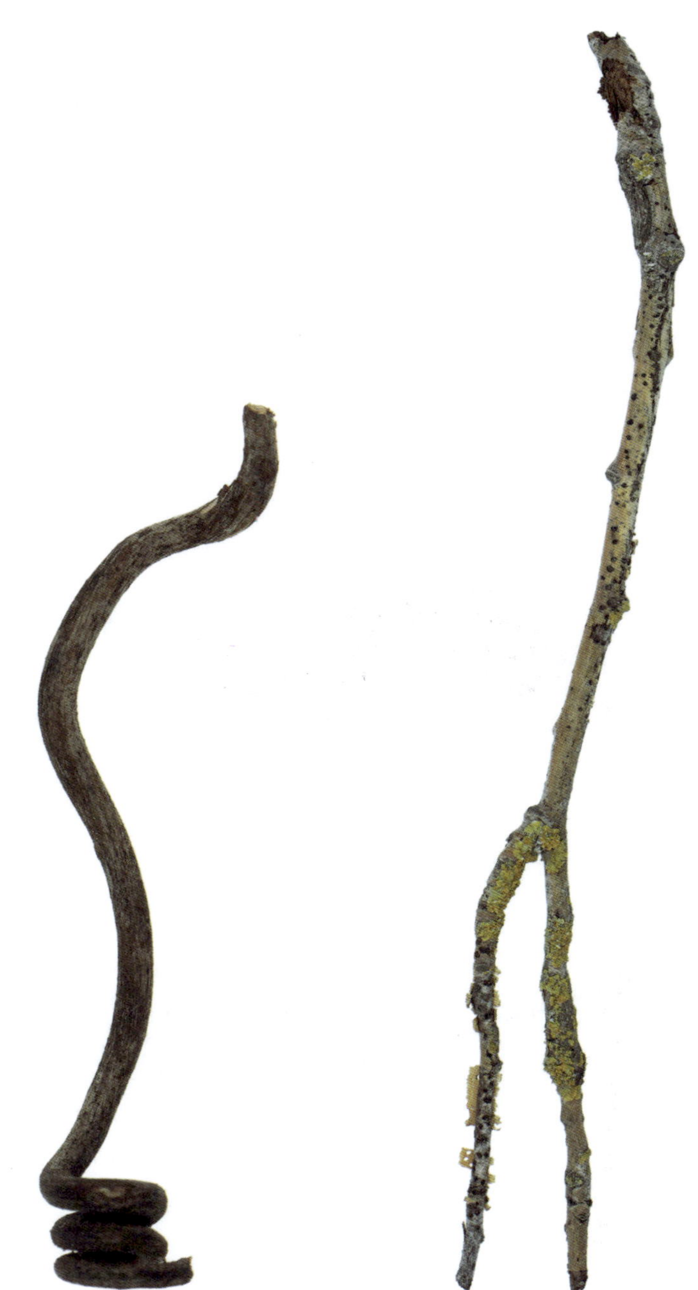

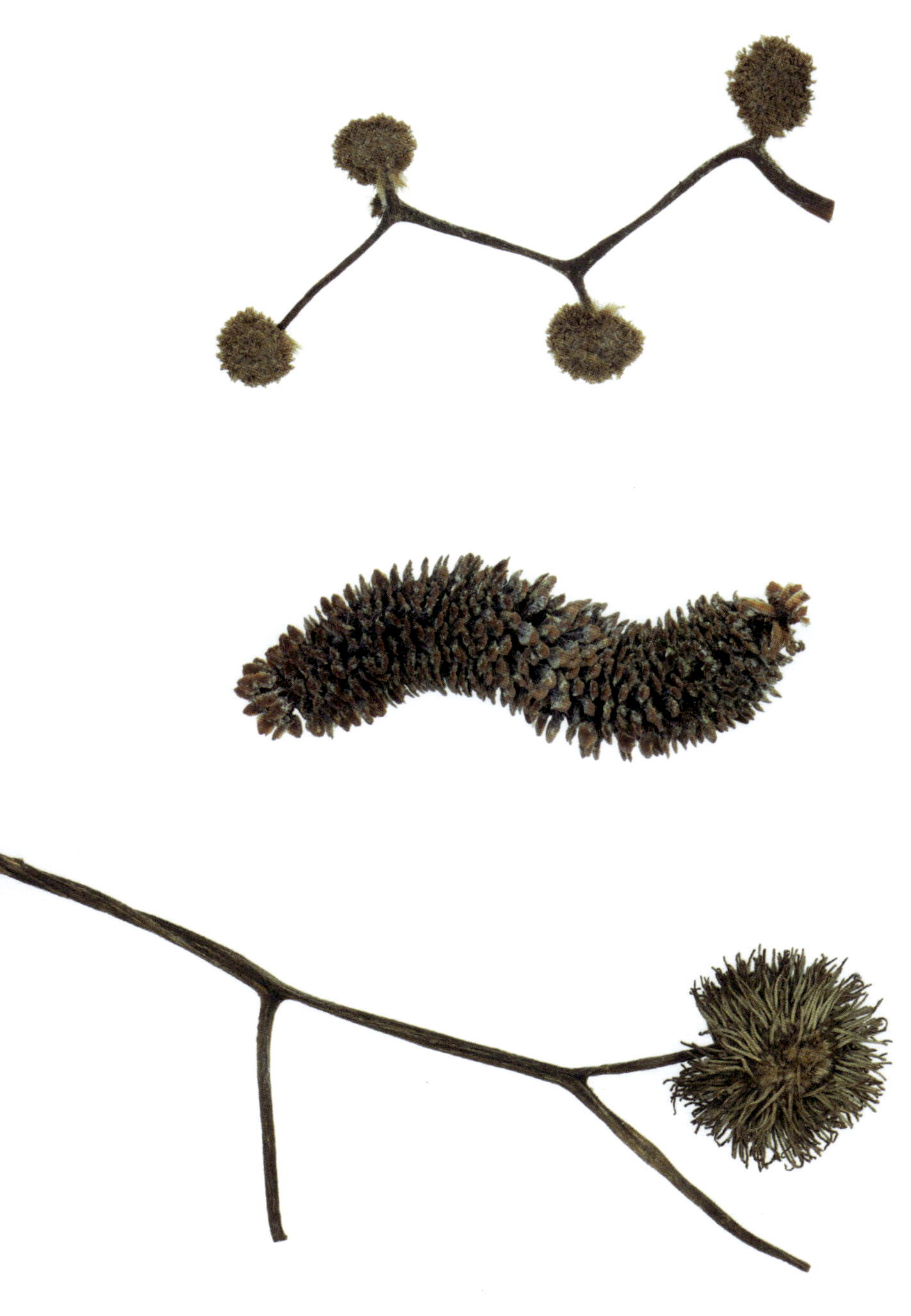

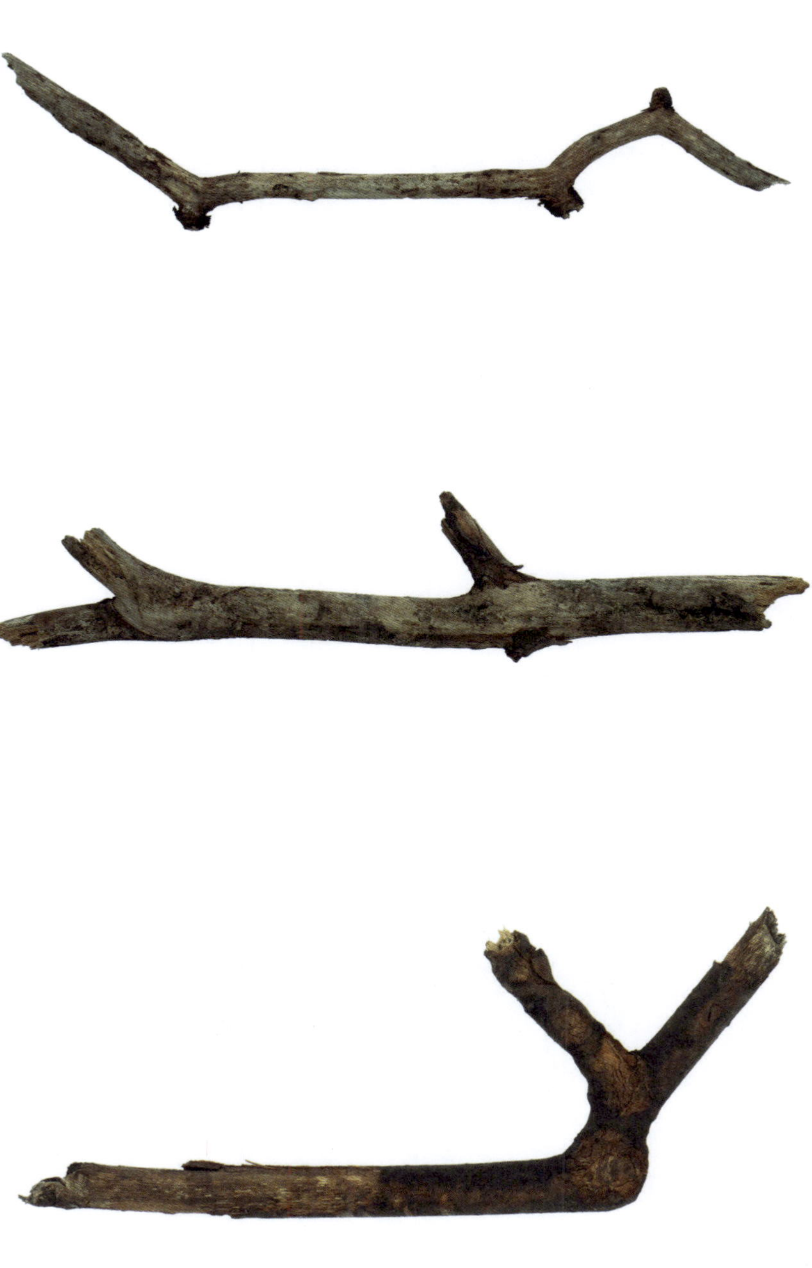

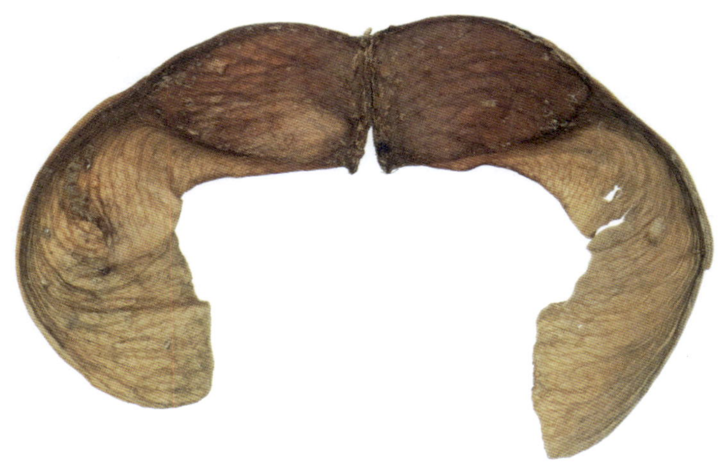
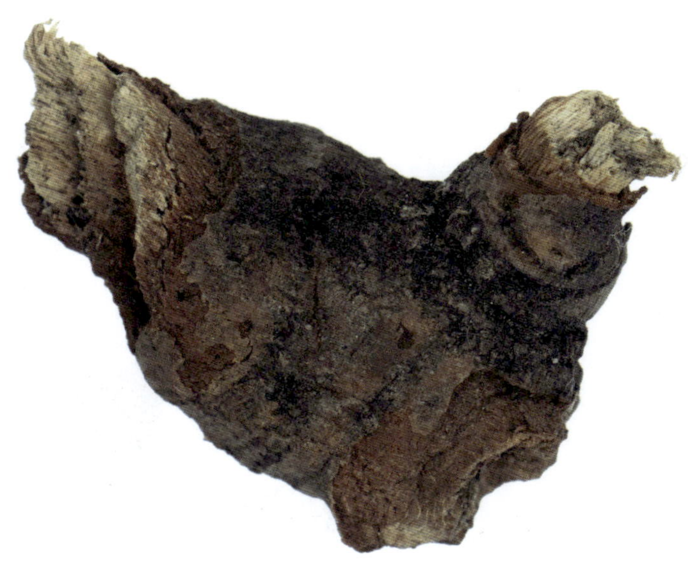

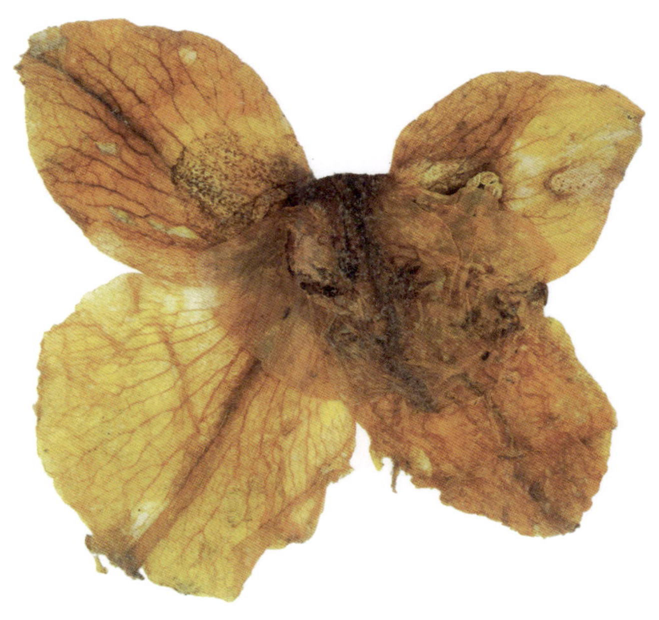

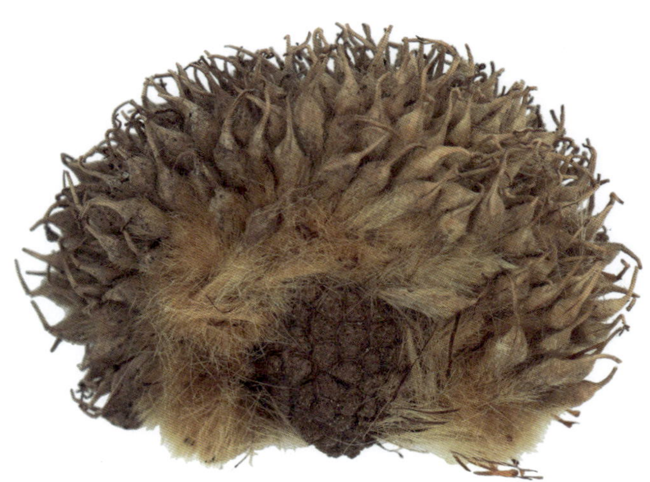

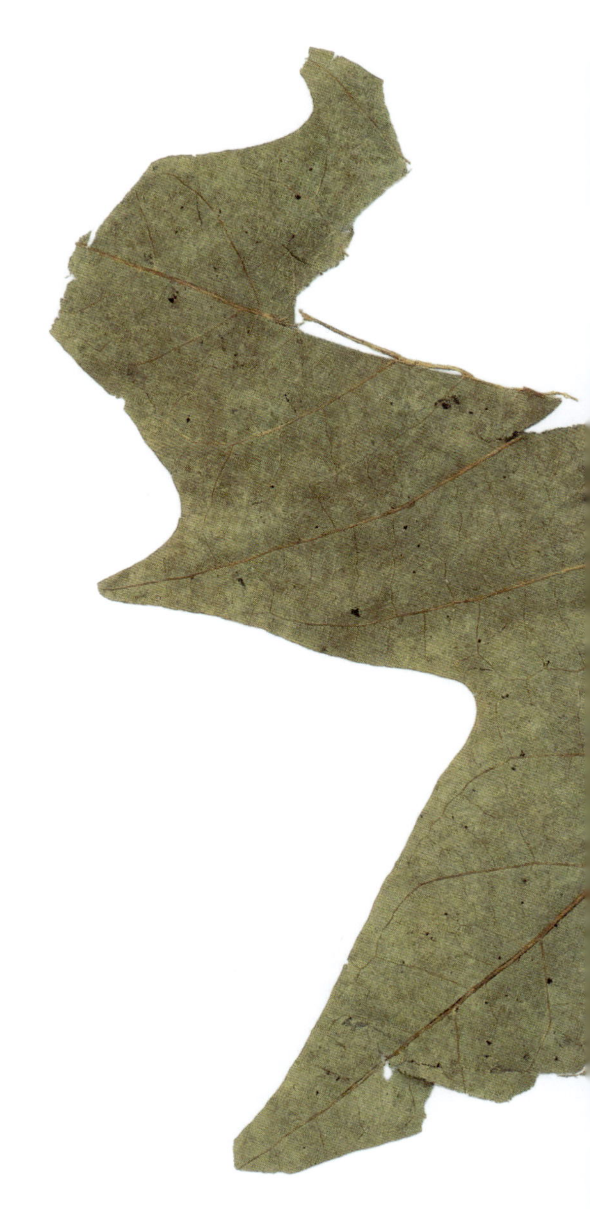

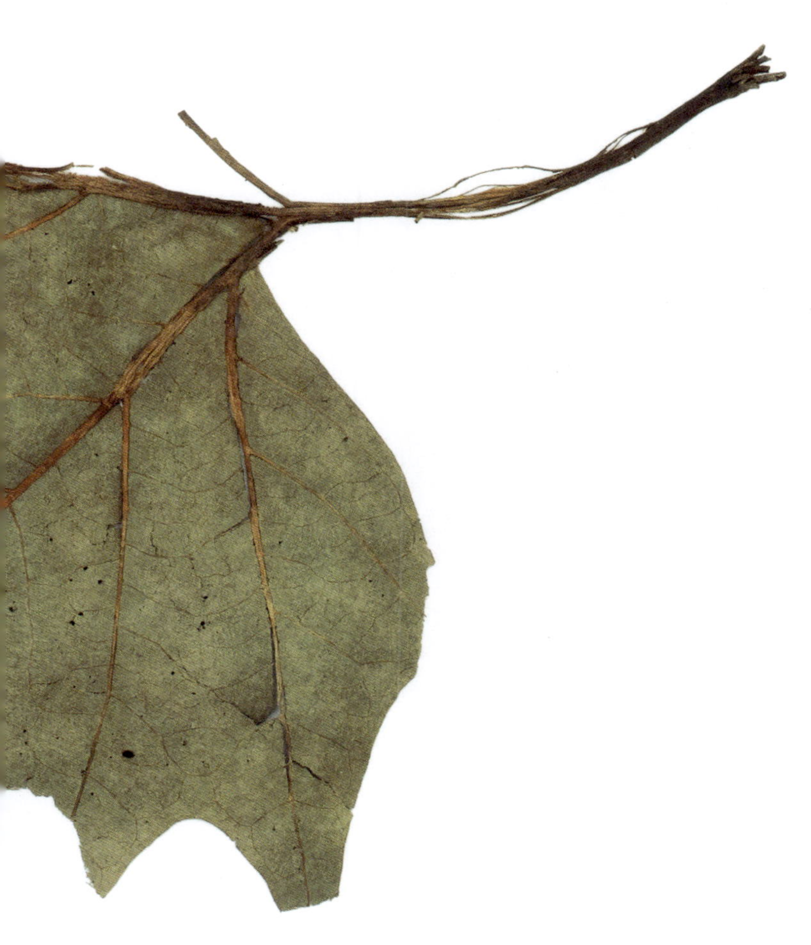

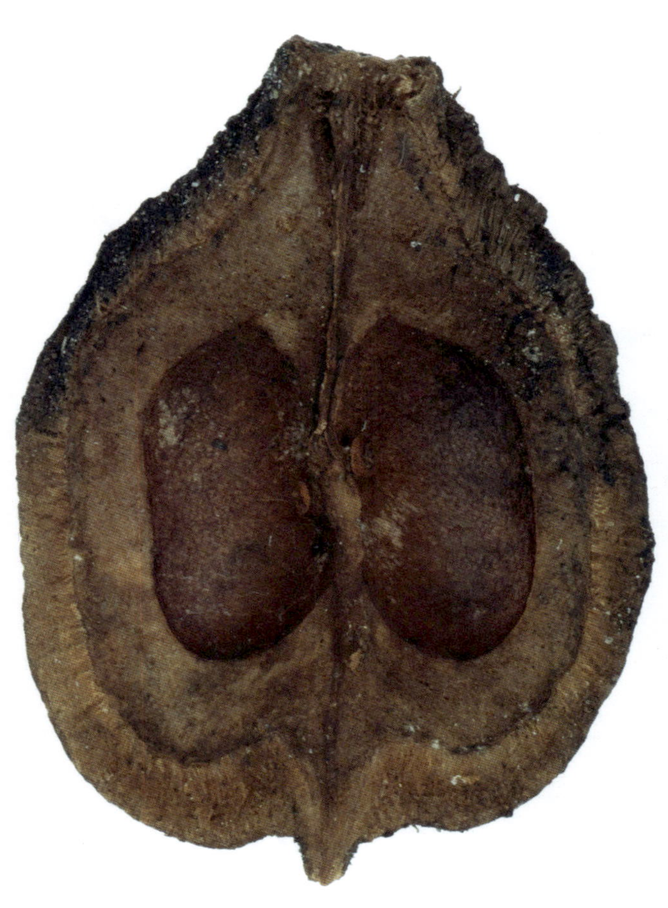